IL CAMPIELLO
a Venetian comedy

Carlo Goldoni
Adaptation by Richard Nelson
from a literal translation by
Erika Gastelli

357 W 20th St., NY NY 10011
212 627-1055

IL CAMPIELLO
© Copyright 1991 by Richard Nelson

First printing: November 1991
ISBN: 0-88145-094-4

Book design: Marie Donovan
Word processing: WordMarc Composer Plus
Typographic controls: Xerox Ventura Publisher 2.0
  P.E.
Typeface: Palatino
Printed on recycled acid-free paper, and bound in the
  USA.

BY RICHARD NELSON
PUBLISHED BY
BROADWAY PLAY PUBLISHING INC

Plays

AN AMERICAN COMEDY (Mark Taper Forum)
BAL (In the anthology ANTI-NATURALISM;
    Goodman Theater)
BETWEEN EAST AND WEST (Hampstead Theatre
    Club, Yale Rep)
JUNGLE COUP (In the anthology PLAYS FROM
    PLAYWRIGHTS HORIZONS)
RIP VAN WINKLE OR "THE WORKS" (Yale Rep)
ROOTS IN WATER (River Arts Rep, BBC Radio 3)

Adaptations

DON JUAN by Molière (Arena Stage)
THE MARRIAGE OF FIGARO by Beaumarchais
    (Guthrie Theater, Broadway)
THREE SISTERS by Chekhov (Guthrie Theater)

ABOUT THE AUTHOR

Richard Nelson's other plays include TWO SHAKESPEAREAN ACTORS (Royal Shakespeare Company), SENSIBILITY AND SENSE (American Playhouse Television), THE END OF A SENTENCE (American Playhouse), PRINCIPIA SCRIPTORIAE (Manhattan Theater Club and the Royal Shakespeare Company), THE RETURN OF PINOCCHIO, THE VIENNA NOTES, CONJURING AN EVENT, and THE KILLING OF YABLONSKI.

His other translations and adaptations include Brecht's JUNGLE OF CITIES and THE WEDDING (BAM Theater Company), Erdman's THE SUICIDE (Arena Stage and The Goodman Theater), and Fo's ACCIDENTAL DEATH OF AN ANARCHIST (Broadway). He also is the author of the book for the Broadway musical CHESS, and numerous radio plays for the BBC.

Nelson has received a London TIME OUT Theatre Award, two Giles Cooper Awards, two Obies, a Guggenheim Fellowship, two Rockefeller Playwriting Grants, two National Endowment for the Arts Playwriting Fellowships, and a Lila Wallace *Reader's Digest* Fund Writer's Award.

ORIGINAL PRODUCTION

IL CAMPIELLO was first performed in Venice during Carnival in 1756. This adaptation was first perfomed on 16 January 1981 at the Lehman College Center by the Acting Company (Margot Harley, Executive Producer) as part of its 1980-1981 Touring Season, with the following cast and creative contributors:

GASPARINA .... Pamela Nyberg
DONNA CATTE .... Michele-Denise Woods
LUCIETTA .... Lori Putnam
DONA PASQUA .... Lynn Chausow
GNESE .... Johann Carlo
ORSOLA .... Laura Smyth
ZORZETTO .... Brian Reddy
ANZOLETTO .... Robert Lovitz
CAVALIER .... Richard Howard
FABRIZIO .... Casey Biggs
SANSUGA .... Jeffrey M Rubin
A boy .... Paul Walker
Townspeople/musicians .... Becky Borczon
        Keven McGuire, Richard S Iglewski, Alan Silver

Director .... Liviu Ciulei
Set designer .... Radu Boruzescu
Costume designer .... Miruna Boruzescu
Lighting designer .... Dennis Parichy
Musical director .... Bruce Adolphe
Choreographer .... Anna Sokolow
Stage manager .... Don Judge

For Liviu

CHARACTERS

GASPARINA, a young, affected woman
DONNA CATTE, a widow
LUCIETTA, her daughter
DONA PASQUA, a widow
GNESE, her daughter
ORSOLA, a hot potato peddler
ZORZETTO, her son
ANZOLETTO, a peddler
CAVALIER
FABRIZIO, GASPARINA's uncle
SANSUGA, a waiter at the inn

Townspeople, a boy, and musicians

NOTE

When the director Liviu Ciulei and I first began to
work on the text of IL CAMPIELLO, he mentioned
an Italian friend who had seen Giorgio Strehler's
production in Milan. "My friend," Liviu told me,
"said that within moments of the first act he began to
cry, and that he never stopped crying throughout."

My single suggestion to anyone who might do IL
CAMPIELLO is to keep in mind that the world of this
play is a profoundly sad one. The *campiello* of the title
is a little square, surrounded by tightly packed
houses—a sort of 18th century Italian slum. The
people here are poor, their opportunities few, if any,
and as such, their passions should never be portrayed
as quaint or cute, but rather as possibly näive. Though
the people of the *campiello* are not aware of the
difficulty of their lives—as they have known nothing
else—that does not mean one should fall into the trap
of idealizing this world. In fact, I believe that it is
precisely the juxtaposition of this harsh reality with
the characters' innocent and honest emotions that
creates the rich texture of the play.

One should hope that an audience will respond to
IL CAMPIELLO in much the same way as one might
respond to watching children play in a ghetto; that is,
as one watches one longs for the children's innocence,
and yet at the same time one is saddened by the
knowledge of what their lives are like and what they
will become. It is this knowledge and longing that

makes us feel sad—both for what they lack and what we have lost; and yet it is also their pleasure and joy and spirit which is so infectious that makes IL CAMPIELLO a comedy as well.

R.N.

ACT ONE

(A campiello [little square]. Venice. Winter. Houses on three sides. To one side is GASPARINA's, which has a balcony. Next to it is LUCIETTA's, which has a smaller balcony. On the other side of the campiello is ORSOLA's house, and next to it is GNESE's. Both have balconies. Upstage center is the inn, which is fronted by a raised terrace.)

(The voice of ZORZETTO shatters the morning quiet. He hawks a kind of numbers game. As he enters, we see him carrying a large basket full of plates, soup dishes, etc.— the prizes of the game. As he enters, the campiello slowly becomes alive—windows, doors open one by one—as the women of the campiello are tempted to try their luck.)

ZORZETTO: Numbers! Numbers! *(Enters)*
Venturina! Venturina!
Who wants to venture with the Venturina?!
One number for one penny,
One penny lets you play,
Who doesn't have one penny?
And what's a penny anyway?
Carnival's here! Carnival's here!
Forget your woes, it's that time of year!
Get out in the winter's sun,
Quick before the day's begun,
Who knows what before we're through,
Someone's got to win so why not you?!
Why not you?! Why not you?! Why not you?!!!

LUCIETTA: *(From her balcony)* Zorzetto! Up here! Catch!

ZORZETTO: *(Catching her penny)* Very nice, Signorina Lucietta. You're the first, so it's your call—high or low?

LUCIETTA: High. High. Bring me luck.

ZORZETTO: I'm sure you'll win. One down, six to go.

GNESE: *(From her balcony)* Zorzi!

ZORZETTO: Good morning, Signorina Gnese.

GNESE: Here's my penny!

ZORZETTO: Throw it.

GNESE: Bring me luck.

ZORZETTO: If only I could. *(Catches her penny)* Two down, five to go.

ORSOLA: *(From her balcony)* Hey, you silly boy! You want my penny or don't you?

ZORZETTO: Yes, Mamma.

ORSOLA: Then take it. Here. *(Throws down her penny)* Wish your mamma luck.

ZORZETTO: I wish my mamma luck. Three down, four to go.

LUCIETTA: Orsola, you're betting?

ORSOLA: Why shouldn't I? What's the call?

LUCIETTA: High. High.

GASPARINA: *(From her balcony)* Come to me, Zorzetto!

ZORZETTO: Coming. Coming, Signorina Gasparina!

GASPARINA: I'm throwing!

ZORZETTO: *(Catches her penny)* Nice throw. Three to go.

PASQUA: *(From the door of her house)* Hey, Zorzetto, what about me? My money's not good enough?

ZORZETTO: I'm all yours, Donna Pasqua.

GNESE: You too, Mamma?

PASQUA: What's wrong? You think I'm too old to have a little fun?

LUCIETTA: Please yourself.

ZORZETTO: Two more! Two more!

CATTE: *(At her door)* Hey you! You with the numbers!

ZORZETTO: *(To himself)* Donna Catte—the chatterbox.

LUCIETTA: Not you too, Signora Mamma?!

CATTE: Yes. Me too. Me too. What's the call?

ZORZETTO: High.

GASPARINA: High? Who called high?

ZORZETTO: High is the call, Signorina.

GASPARINA: Why wasn't I told? Had I known, I might not have played.

LUCIETTA: Oh, too bad.

GASPARINA: *(To herself)* It's always got to be her way.

LUCIETTA: *(To ZORZETTO)* Come on, let's draw! What are you waiting for?

ZORZETTO: For one more bettor, Signorina. It's unlucky to draw with less than seven. Unless someone wishes to bet twice?

LUCIETTA: I will!

GASPARINA: I will! I've got a penny here! Here, take it! Take it! *(Throws down her penny)*

LUCIETTA: Pushy cow.

GNESE: She thinks she's something all right.

ORSOLA: Let's draw! I don't have all day.

ZORZETTO: Everyone knows the call is high?

LUCIETTA: I'll draw first, Zorzetto.

GASPARINA: No, me first!

LUCIETTA: You think you're such a bigshot. I bet first so I pick first!

GASPARINA: But my dear, I bet twice!

PASQUA: My daughter's the youngest, she should go first!

ZORZETTO: I'm not getting in the middle of this.

ORSOLA: Zorzi, your mamma should go first!

ZORZETTO: (Throwing her the satchel) Draw! Draw! What does it matter who goes first?!

GASPARINA: Such nerve!

ORSOLA: What's wrong? You think I'm not good enough to go first?

GASPARINA: You said it, I didn't.

ORSOLA: You have no right to say that to me. I make an honest living.

GASPARINA: If it doesn't bother you to run through the street peddling your hot potatoes, yelling like a beggar....

ZORZETTO: Come on. Come on. Draw!

ORSOLA: (To GASPARINA) Who do you think you are?

GASPARINA: My dear, I am who I am.

LUCIETTA: And that is why we laugh at you.

GNESE: What a character!

GASPARINA: Jealous?

LUCIETTA: Don't make me laugh!

ZORZETTO: Are you going to draw or aren't you?

GASPARINA: My father was a respectable man! He was a gentleman, even a nobleman! That's who my father was! And if my mamma was a simple seamstress, that doesn't change the fact that my father was a gentleman! You—*(Points to* GNESE*)* yours made shoes! And yours—*(Points to* LUCIETTA*)* he peddled fruits!

CATTE: So he peddled fruit. But he was good at peddling fruit.

GASPARINA: Good? Then why did he end up roasting chestnuts in the piazza?!!

PASQUA: Yes, my husband, God bless him, was a shoemaker, but for him shoemaking was an art and everyone knows that!!!

ZORZETTO: Are you going to draw or not?!!

ORSOLA: How she goes on about herself. I'm drawing. I'm drawing. *(Draws from the sack, tosses sack and marker back to* ZORZETTO*)* There. What did I get?

ZORZETTO: Number sixty.

ORSOLA: Is that good or bad?

ZORZETTO: I don't know yet.

GASPARINA: Too low. Much too low. Too bad.

ORSOLA: *(To* GASPARINA*)* Big mouth!

ZORZETTO: You're next, Signorina Gnese.

GASPARINA: *(To herself)* I knew she'd be next. She's his girlfriend.

GNESE: *(Draws)* Oh, I got the star!

(Throws back the satchel and marker)

ZORZETTO: Very nice. Very nice. The star. That counts as eighty. Your turn, Donna Pasqua.

GASPARINA: *(To herself)* Figures. First the girl, then her mother. Sucking up to both of them.

PASQUA: What did I draw?

ZORZETTO: Death.

PASQUA: Oh. That's not very good, is it? What does death count for?

ZORZETTO: Death? Nothing.

CATTE: That's a shame.

ZORZETTO: *(To* CATTE*)* Your turn.

CATTE: Bring it over here. *(Draws)* What does it say? I don't have my glasses.

ZORZETTO: The devil.

GNESE: Too bad.

CATTE: Does that mean I don't win?

ZORZETTO: I wouldn't get your hopes up.

LUCIETTA: Me next! Me next!

(She's thrown the satchel.)

GASPARINA: I'll go last.

ZORZETTO: The star's the one to beat!

GNESE: That's me. I got the star!

PASQUA: Looks good for my daughter.

LUCIETTA: *(Draws)* The moon! I picked the moon!

CATTE: Looks better for mine.

ZORZETTO: Come on. Come on. The moon's now the one to beat. That counts as ninety.

GASPARINA: My turn.

ZORZETTO: Here you are.

GNESE: I feel like banging my head against a wall.

ZORZETTO: Go ahead, pick.

GASPARINA: What did I get?

ZORZETTO: Number seventy.

LUCIETTA: I won! I won!

GASPARINA: Not so fast. I get another pick.

LUCIETTA: I'm going to win. I'm going to win.

GASPARINA: What did I pick?

ZORZETTO: The sun! She's picked the sun and that counts as a hundred!

GASPARINA: I win! I win!

LUCIETTA: Bitch. She always wins.

ZORZETTO: What will it be, Gasparina? A plate?

GASPARINA: No, I'll take a soup bowl.

ZORZETTO: Then a soup bowl it shall be.

GASPARINA: Wait! This morning I'm going to break all of you. Come on, let's play again. This time for low.

LUCIETTA: I quit. I have a headache.

GASPARINA: Since when?

LUCIETTA: Since now!

(Goes into her house)

GNESE: I better go too.

GASPARINA: Gnese, you aren't leaving?

GNESE: Why? Do I need to ask your permission?

(Goes into her house)

ORSOLA: Get inside, Son. The game's over. *(Looks up)* Going to rain.

GASPARINA: The fun's over?

ORSOLA: Yes!

(Goes into her house)

GASPARINA: If that's how you want it, then see if I care!!! How dare they treat me like this?! Don't they realize who I am?!! Someday I'll show them!

ZORZETTO: Here's your soup bowl.

GASPARINA: Keep it. What do I want with a soup bowl? I have better bowls than that. *(Turns to go in, stops)* Compared to all of them, I am the sun!!!!

(Goes inside)

ZORZETTO: *(To young BOY who has entered)* Boy, give me a hand with this basket and I'll give you a penny. (BOY *helps him.)* That leaves six pennies for me. All in all not a bad take. I should invest them wisely; what should it be? Three dumplings or two pieces of cake?

(Leaves with the BOY)

(DONNA PASQUA and DONNA CATTE appear at their doors.)

PASQUA: So?

CATTE: So what?

PASQUA: So what do you think about Gasparina having all the luck this morning?

CATTE: She was born lucky. What can you do?

PASQUA: I remember her mother. Day in, day out she'd come to my door. It was always something. Salt, one day; oil, the next. Poor as dirt. Dead now. And here's her daughter living like there's no tomorrow.

CATTE: Do you think the old man living with her is really her uncle?

PASQUA: Who knows? Though one hears talk.

CATTE: Who is he then? What have you heard?

PASQUA: I don't want to gossip. It's none of our business who he is.

CATTE: Yes, it's none of our business who he is. It's a shame to have my daughter exposed to that sort of thing.

PASQUA: Oh I wouldn't worry about your daughter. She's old enough. But mine, the poor child, she's not even sixteen.

CATTE: So how old do you think my child is?

PASQUA: I don't know. Twenty-one? Twenty-two?

CATTE: That just shows how deceptive looks can fool you. She's not even eighteen. It's the same with me. I'm not nearly as old as I look. It's the worrying that does it.

PASQUA: How old do you think I am?

CATTE: You? I'd say, somewhere between sixty and seventy.

PASQUA: Don't be stupid! Everyone knows you're as blind as a bat.

CATTE: Then how old are you?

PASQUA: Forty-three.

CATTE: Forty-three? I never would have guessed. How old do you think I am?

PASQUA: Sixty. Maybe a little more.

CATTE: Sixty! My dear, the truth is I am younger than you.

PASQUA: But you've no teeth!

CATTE: Because of an inflammation. If only you'd seen me when I was young!

PASQUA: What?

CATTE: Are you deaf?

PASQUA: Only in this ear.

CATTE: Dear heart, I'd rather not make a big deal over this, but you are older.

PASQUA: You wouldn't say that if you knew how I've suffered. My husband, God forgive him.

CATTE: Husbands. Yes. They are the death of all of us. Complain. Complain.

PASQUA: Never happy. If it wasn't one thing, then it was my cooking. He had his nerve. God rest his soul.

CATTE: Not to boast, but if you had only seen me when I was young! But without teeth, what can you do? Feel here. I've got two left. Here's one. *(Puts* PASQUA's *finger in her mouth)* There. Can you feel the roots? Here's the big one. I had wonderful teeth.

PASQUA: Do you find it hard to chew?

CATTE: Not when there's something worth chewing.

PASQUA: The same with me.

CATTE: Which isn't every day.

PASQUA: What?

CATTE: I thought it was the other ear.

PASQUA: It is. Though this one's a little deaf too. Come in for a minute.

CATTE: No. I should go see what that girl of mine is up to. She worries me.

PASQUA: I'll bet you'd like to see her married.

CATTE: What mother wouldn't?

PASQUA: What about the peddler?

CATTE: If he'll have her. What about yours?

PASQUA: Don't breathe a word of this, but I have my eye on Orsola's son. Though I wish he were a little older.

CATTE: He's getting older every day.

PASQUA: But so is she. To tell you the truth, I wouldn't mind getting her off my hands, what with me thinking of getting married again.

CATTE: You? Me too. Soon as I get mine out of the house.

PASQUA: Get them settled so we can start thinking about ourselves for a change.

CATTE: The sooner the better.

PASQUA: The sooner the better.

CATTE: There's no point in fooling myself. I'm not as young as I once was. But I still expect to bury at least one more husband before I'm through.

(Goes inside)

PASQUA: I may be a little deaf, but I still have my figure. So there's the little problem with the ear, but the rest of me's still in one piece.

(Goes inside)

(GASPARINA enters on her balcony.)

GASPARINA: What a day! Such a beautiful day as this was meant to be enjoyed! I'd give anything to get out, but I'd never get my stupid uncle to come with me. He's glued to his stupid books. It's always them before me. I'll never get married at this rate. There is that gentleman who's been staying at the inn. He's always bowing at me. I wonder who he is. No one knows. (CAVALIER *enters from the inn.*) Oh, my God, it's him!

(CAVALIER, *affecting a swagger, approaches* GASPARINA'*s house. He bows to her.*)

(GASPARINA *curtsies.*)

(CAVALIER *swaggers around a bit more, then bows to her again.*)

(GASPARINA *curtsies again.*)

(CAVALIER *swaggers some more, then, smiling, he kisses his hand as a gesture to* GASPARINA.)

(GASPARINA *answers by gracefully kissing her own hand.*)

(CAVALIER *walks toward the inn, stops, hesitates, then returns, obviously wishing to speak with her; then thinks better of it, bows, and walks back toward the inn. At the door he stops, kisses his hand yet again, and enters the inn.*)

GASPARINA: He likes me! There's no question that he likes me. He acted like he did. That is, if I can trust the way he acted, then there's no question that he likes me. He seems to like me. I wonder if he likes me. If he does, they're going to be so jealous, they won't know what to do.

(SANSUGA *enters, shaking his head.*)

SANSUGA: Foreigners! The things they ask. Still, what can you do? You can't say no. So—I'll talk to her, if that's what he wants. I'm just the waiter at the inn, so I'm here to please. (*To* GASPARINA) Excuse me, Signorina.

GASPARINA: Yes?

SANSUGA: The gentleman who was just here, did you see him?

GASPARINA: Yes. Who is he?

SANSUGA: A cavalier.

GASPARINA: No?! Really?

SANSUGA: He fancies you.

GASPARINA: How dare you talk to me like this!

SANSUGA: Like what?

GASPARINA: Do you know who I am?

SANSUGA: Yes. I know who you are.

GASPARINA: Then you know one does not speak to me like this.

SANSUGA: He just wants to meet you.

GASPARINA: Meet me? Why didn't he ask me himself?

SANSUGA: Don't ask me to understand the mind of a foreigner. I'm just a waiter, I have enough to do.

GASPARINA: Tell him I shall greet him.

SANSUGA: You'll greet him?

GASPARINA: Yes.

SANSUGA: This gentleman? Does he interest you?

GASPARINA: I've seen better. But I've also seen worse.

SANSUGA: I'll go tell him.

GASPARINA: Wait! Does he know I am available for marriage?

SANSUGA: He knows.

GASPARINA: Wait! Does he know that I'm an honest girl, who just happens to be poor?

SANSUGA: He knows. He knows. Now just stay there. Don't move.

GASPARINA: I shall stay.

(SANSUGA *exits into the inn.*)

GASPARINA: Oh God, it's awful! To think that
someone like me should not have a dowry! Think of
it! It's not fair. It's not fair! That uncle of mine arrives
out of nowhere and keeps asking: "Niece, shouldn't
you be thinking of marriage?" Well, do I disagree? I
agree! I agree! But has he put a penny aside? I don't
know. I don't even know if he has a penny *to* put
aside. *(She hears something.)* It's him. He's calling.
What a time to pick. He doesn't like it when I stay
out here. How he ever expects me to meet anybody,
I have no idea. I can't spend the rest of my life waiting
on him. I'd end up like a mouldy pear.

(She goes inside.)

(LUCIETTA enters onto her balcony.)

LUCIETTA: Still no sign of Anzoletto. Three hours
I've been waiting for that boy. He's usually here long
before now. Men. Men. There never was a man who
could be trusted.

(CAVALIER enters. He looks toward GASPARINA's house.)

LUCIETTA: Why's he looking over here? What does he
want with me?

CAVALIER: It looks like her, but then again....

LUCIETTA: He's looking at me.

(CAVALIER takes off his hat, hesitates.)

LUCIETTA: *(Curtsies)* Sir....

*(CAVALIER completes his bow, then looks at her through
his monocle.)*

LUCIETTA: He's having trouble seeing me.

CAVALIER: No, not the same one. But then again, she's
also my type. *(Looks through his monocle)*

LUCIETTA: If he keeps staring at me like I'm
something for sale, I'll break his face.

(CAVALIER *bows.*)

LUCIETTA: And to you. *(Curtsies and blows him a raspberry)*

CAVALIER: I'm sorry, I didn't catch that.

LUCIETTA: *(Curtsies)* Sir.... *(Blows a raspberry)*

CAVALIER: Come again. I'm having a hard time understanding you.

(ANZOLETTO *enters with his boxes of notions.*)

ANZOLETTO: Ribbons! Braids! Flanders lace!

LUCIETTA: *(Calling)* Anzoletto!

ANZOLETTO: You! I caught you!

CAVALIER: Signorina, allow me to buy you something.

LUCIETTA: Thank you, Sir. Don't worry about him. Stay there. I'll come down. *(She goes inside.)*

CAVALIER: Young man....

ANZOLETTO: Sir....

CAVALIER: Whatever she wants, give it to her. I'll pay.

ANZOLETTO: *(To himself)* Whore! Whore!

(GNESE *enters on her balcony.*)

GNESE: *(To* ANZOLETTO*)* Hey you! Come here!

CAVALIER: What? Hm. She too is my type.

GNESE: You got any pretty ribbons?

CAVALIER: Give her what she wants. I'll pay.

GNESE: Is he serious?

CAVALIER: Of course. Whatever you desire. Just choose.

GNESE: Peddler, come upstairs.

ANZOLETTO: Coming. Coming.

(Enters her house)

CAVALIER: So many beautiful creatures. It's like a dream. *(To* GNESE*)* Just help yourself!

GENSE: I'll only take what I need. *(She goes inside.)*

*(*LUCIETTA *enters from her door.)*

LUCIETTA: Can't he wait one second without running off to her?!

CAVALIER: Patience, my dear, he'll be back.

LUCIETTA: Patience, that's easy for you to say. *(To herself)* Who the hell is this man anyway?

CAVALIER: May I ask your name?

LUCIETTA: My name? Lucietta? *(To herself)* How dare he do this to me?!!

CAVALIER: Lucietta.

LUCIETTA: What? What do you want?

CAVALIER: Are you married, Lucietta?

LUCIETTA: No.

CAVALIER: Then you are unmarried?

LUCIETTA: Yes, I am unmarried. But I don't plan to stay that way.

CAVALIER: May I come down to you?

LUCIETTA: Who's stopping you?

*(*CAVALIER *goes inside.)*

LUCIETTA: *(In the direction of* ANZOLETTO*)* I hope he sees me talking to this foreigner. That'll get his goat. Who does he think he is leaving me like that?!!!

CATTE: *(Off)* Lucietta!

LUCIETTA: She can shout her head off, but I'm not moving 'til I tell that bastard a thing or two.

CATTE: *(Entering)* What are you doing out in the street?

LUCIETTA: Nothing.

CATTE: What happened? What's wrong?

LUCIETTA: *(Crying)* That son of a bitch.... He walked away from me.... I asked him to wait...but he didn't!

CATTE: And that's why you're crying?

LUCIETTA: Yes.

CATTE: He'll come back. They always do.

(CAVALIER enters.)

CAVALIER: Here I am.

CATTE: *(To LUCIETTA)* Who's he?

LUCIETTA: *(To CATTE)* Sh-sh. Shut up.

CAVALIER: Who's the old woman?

LUCIETTA: She's my mamma.

CATTE: Who's he calling an old woman? I think he needs glasses.

CAVALIER: I beg your pardon. It was your daughter's beauty that blinded me.

CATTE: Yes, you're right, she's a very lovely girl. She gets it from me.

CAVALIER: That is obvious to me now. Ladies, when the peddler returns, allow me to pay for whatever you wish.

(GNESE enters on her balcony.)

GNESE: I bought four lira's worth!

CAVALIER: Only four? Why stop there? I'm paying!

GNESE: I've paid! Venetian girls are good girls, and good girls don't take presents from strangers! *(Goes inside)*

*(*ANZOLETTO *enters from the house.)*

CAVALIER: Ah. This one is not my type at all. Too much the heroine. *(To* LUCIETTA*)* What are you waiting for? Go. Go. Whatever you want is yours!

LUCIETTA: I don't want anything! *(To* ANZOLETTO*)* Get away from me. You...you bastard!

ANZOLETTO: You have your nerve yelling at me, I'm the one who should be yelling!

LUCIETTA: This isn't the place to deal with you. But you just wait!

ANZOLETTO: No, you just wait!

CATTE: *(To* ANZOLETTO*)* Enough. Enough. Come inside.

ANZOLETTO: You couldn't drag me in there! *(Leaves)*

CAVALIER: Thank God, he's gone. Allow me to offer you this ring, my dear, as a tribute to your beauty.

LUCIETTA: I'm sorry. No. *(Leaves)*

CATTE: Foreigner. You. Come here.

CAVALIER: What do you want?

CATTE: As her mother, I'll accept the ring.

CAVALIER: Bless you. Here, take it. Though remember to mention me when you give it to her. Thank you, dear lady. Thank you. *(Leaves)*

CATTE: Who said anything about giving it to her? She's too young to appreciate such things. Besides, it'll come in handy when I get engaged. *(Leaves)*

END OF ACT ONE

ACT TWO

(DONNA PASQUA *enters from her house with a broom.*)

PASQUA: Look at this square. It's full of garbage. I just don't understand how people can be so thoughtless. They're worse than children. Fishbones. Half-chewed biscuits. Just thrown down on the ground. It makes you sick. Does anyone besides me ever think to clean up this mess? If it weren't for me.... I suppose they don't want to wear out their brooms.

(*Sweeps in front of her house*)

ORSOLA: (*At her balcony*) Donna Pasqua?! Hey, Donna Pasqua! Poor thing. Deaf as a slug. I said—hey, Donna Pasqua!!

PASQUA: What? Who's calling?

ORSOLA: Donna Pasqua, I was wondering since you've got your broom out would you mind giving the front of my house a little sweep?

PASQUA: What do you think I am? Do it yourself.

ORSOLA: Oh, of course. We wouldn't want the Madonna to strain herself.

PASQUA: (*To herself*) Who does she think she is?

ORSOLA: It's not like I'm asking for a million lira.

PASQUA: (*To herself*) Give her an inch and she'll take a mile.

ORSOLA: Is it such a big deal to sweep a few more feet?

PASQUA: What? *(To herself)* I can't hear what she's saying.

ORSOLA: I'm saying is it wrong to help a neighbor?

PASQUA: What? Who did what to what neighbor?

ORSOLA: God you are deaf. Poor thing.

PASQUA: Deaf? Who's deaf? Just this morning my hearing was perfect. Then I got an attack of inflammation. The wind does it to me.

ORSOLA: Pasqua, listen to me.

PASQUA: Listen to what? *(Gets closer)*

ORSOLA: You're my friend, right?

PASQUA: I am. But that doesn't make me your servant.

ORSOLA: Of course. You're quite right. Tell me, where's your daughter?

PASQUA: Inside. She's working. Lately, you can't pull her away from her work.

ORSOLA: A girl after my own heart.

PASQUA: She's a good girl.

(Starts to sweep in front of ORSOLA'*s house)*

ORSOLA: Oh, don't bother with that.

PASQUA: She's not at all like some of the others.

ORSOLA: No, she's a good girl.

PASQUA: And she's also not ugly.

ORSOLA: Not ugly! Good God, she is a flower! Your daughter's a beautiful blossoming flower!

*(*PASQUA *sweeps harder.)*

ORSOLA: Please, don't trouble yourself. You'll embarrass me.

PASQUA: And industrious. Very industrious is that daughter of mine.

ORSOLA: When do you think she'll get married?

PASQUA: If only I knew! There's the problem with her dowry.

ORSOLA: What problem is that?

PASQUA: She doesn't have any.

ORSOLA: Someone like her shouldn't need a dowry to get a man.

PASQUA: What?

ORSOLA: I said—why don't you come inside where we can talk?

PASQUA: What did you say before?

ORSOLA: She's a beautiful girl. Who knows what could happen.

PASQUA: You think...?

ORSOLA: Come in. Come in. Let's talk about it.

PASQUA: *(To herself)* Maybe we can work out something with her son. I'm coming. I'll be right there. *(Calls)* Gnese!!!

GNESE: *(On her balcony)* What do you want, Mamma?

PASQUA: I'm going in with Signora Orsola. I won't be long.

GNESE: Greetings, Signora Donna Orsola.

ORSOLA: Greetings, my child.

PASQUA: *(To ORSOLA)* What do you say? Beautiful, isn't she? *(To herself)* I looked just like her once. But who knows, maybe I will again—once I get myself remarried.

ORSOLA: Gnese, you are well, I hope?

GNESE: Oh yes.

ORSOLA: What have you been working on?

GNESE: I sew flowers for women's hair.

ORSOLA: The ones made out of velvet?

GNESE: Those. And also those made out of down.

ORSOLA: Can I see?

GNESE: Here.

ORSOLA: Gorgeous. Very gorgeous. Oh yes. Do you sell them to the millinery shop?

GNESE: Are you kidding?! People order direct from me. You'd have to be crazy to sell to the millinery shop. I used to work through them, but all they'd do was complain. They pay twenty cents a flower then turn around and sell them for forty. So now I use a lot of cheap scraps and by selling 'em myself I make a lot more.

ORSOLA: What about bonnets? Can you make them too?

GNESE: Of course.

ORSOLA: Really? A smart girl like you could even open her own shop, I'll bet.

GNESE: But it's hard to begin anything, when you're still single.

ORSOLA: Then get married.

GNESE: If only it were that simple.

ORSOLA: Look, child, take my advice—a good thing doesn't come along every day, so when it does, grab it. I now want to speak to your mother.

(Goes inside)

GNESE: *(Alone)* My mother wants to marry me off. And me too. I want to marry me off too. And I would in a second, but all the men I know are bastards.

LUCIETTA: *(On her balcony)* You make me sick!

GNESE: Me? What did I do?

LUCIETTA: And I thought you were my friend!

GNESE: What did I do?

LUCIETTA: Everybody knows Anzoletto's mine! So what were you doing taking him into your house?!!

GNESE: I bought some things.

LUCIETTA: Bull! He doesn't have to go all the way inside just so you can buy some things!

GNESE: I was too embarrassed to come to the door.

LUCIETTA: Since when have you been too embarrassed to strut out on the street?!

GNESE: When I'm with my mamma, I'm not, but when I'm alone....

LUCIETTA: Listen to me, because I'll only say this once—keep your slimy hands off that boy!

GNESE: I didn't touch him.

LUCIETTA: You want to know what I think of you?

GNESE: Wait. Can't we be friends?

LUCIETTA: I doubt it.

GNESE: Look, I'll give you a flower.

LUCIETTA: Sure.

GNESE: No, I will. Send someone to get it.

LUCIETTA: Who? There's no one here, I'll come myself. No, wait a minute. *(Calls)* Zorzetto!

(ZORZETTO *enters on the street.*)

ZORZETTO: What do you want?

LUCIETTA: I want you to do me a little favor.

ZORZETTO: Sure.

LUCIETTA: Over there, Gnese will give you a flower, bring it back to me.

ZORZETTO: Gladly. *(To* GNESE*)* Here I am. Throw it down.

GNESE: No.

ZORZETTO: Then I should come up?

GNESE: No! I'll lower the basket; let Lucietta pick.

ZORZETTO: They're beautiful. As beautiful as their maker.

GNESE: Shut up!

LUCIETTA: What did he do?

ZORZETTO: *(To* GNESE*)* I thought you loved me.

GNESE: Don't make me laugh.

ZORZETTO: But we've played together since we were children.

GNESE: Children don't know any better.

LUCIETTA: Though maybe now that you're big, look at me Gnese, maybe now you're just playing a different game.

GNESE: *(To* ZORZETTO*)* I told you to give her the flower!

ZORZETTO: I am. I am. What have I done?

GNESE: Get away! Get away!

(She goes inside.)

LUCIETTA: She's in love with you.

ZORZETTO: Maybe once but not any more.

LUCIETTA: No. Now more than ever. When she was a girl, she felt things but didn't think about them, now she both feels and thinks and that's enough to mess up anyone.

ZORZETTO: Well it's messing me up.

LUCIETTA: Bring me the flower. Come up. Come up.

ZORZETTO: I'm coming. I wanted to talk to you anyway.

LUCIETTA: Look at you: You've grown up yourself. How old are you now?

ZORZETTO: Seventeen. Almost seventeen.

LUCIETTA: I have a cousin who was married at fifteen.

ZORZETTO: So?!!

LUCIETTA: So nothing, you silly boy. Come up.

ZORZETTO: I'm coming.

(As he starts to enter her house, ANZOLETTO *enters on the street.)*

ANZOLETTO: *(Pushing* ZORZETTO*)* You little scum!

LUCIETTA: What's happening?!!

ZORZETTO: What did I do?

ANZOLETTO: I'll slam your face in!

ZORZETTO: What for?

LUCIETTA: What's happening?!!

ANZOLETTO: Now you listen to me, if I ever again catch you within ten feet of this door....

ZORZETTO: This door? You don't understand, I was bringing her a flower. Here, then, you give it to her! *(Throws flower on the ground)*

ANZOLETTO: A flower? You bastard!!

ZORZETTO: Mamma! Mamma! He's hurting me!
Mamma!

(ORSOLA *appears on her balcony.*)

ORSOLA: What's going on down there? Hey, leave
my boy alone! Stop that! You want me to come down
there and box your ears in?!!

LUCIETTA: Quiet. Sh-sh. Quiet.

ANZOLETTO: I don't want to see that punk even
looking at you!

ZORZETTO: Who wants to look at her?

ORSOLA: *(Nodding to* LUCIETTA*)* She's always the cause
of trouble.

LUCIETTA: I'm getting tired of all this, Anzoletto!

ORSOLA: I can't take this campiello anymore. Your
kind is destroying it for all of us!

LUCIETTA: What did you say?

ORSOLA: You heard what I said.

LUCIETTA: You have your nerve. You—you, potato
peddler!

ANZOLETTO: *(To* LUCIETTA*)* Shut up!

ORSOLA: Filth!

ANZOLETTO: *(To* ORSOLA*)* Cow, you'll get yours.

ZORZETTO: *(Pushing up against* ANZOLETTO*)* Try it!
I dare you!

ANZOLETTO: Brush off, piss ass.

ORSOLA: Both of you, leave my boy alone!

LUCIETTA: Oh you don't have to worry about that.
Who'd want to have anything to do with such a baby!

There must be something better to do in this town.
Look at the big muscle man! He's all yours, Gnese,
and good riddance!

GNESE: *(Appears on her balcony)* Did I hear my name?

LUCIETTA: You hear Anzoletto and you come running!

GNESE: Watch your mouth!

ORSOLA: Zorzetto, get in here!

ZORZETTO: I'm not moving.

ORSOLA: How dare you talk to your mamma like that!!

ZORZETTO: This time, I stay!

ORSOLA: I'm telling you to get in here!

LUCIETTA: What a big boy!

ORSOLA: You better watch it, you flirt!

(DONNA CATTE enters on the street.)

CATTE: Hey, that's my daughter you're talking to!

ORSOLA: She gets what she deserves!

CATTE: My daughter's not like that; but that's not to
say there aren't those like that in this campiello, but
my daughter's not one of them! She's a good girl!

GNESE: So who's like that?

CATTE: I don't think you'd want me to mention any
names.

GNESE: You...! You...!

(PASQUA enters from her house.)

PASQUA: *(To CATTE)* What have you been saying to
my daughter?!

CATTE: I think I hit a nerve.

GNESE: Mamma, get inside!

PASQUA: What's going on here!!

(CAVALIER *enters.*)

CAVALIER: What's all the shouting about?!!

ANZOLETTO: What's it to you?

CAVALIER: I thought I might be of some help.

ANZOLETTO: Then just tell me one thing—that girl there —(*Points to* LUCIETTA) are you after her?

CAVALIER: No. Not at all.

LUCIETTA: Now do you believe me, Anzoletto?

CAVALIER: Ladies, I respect all women; their cheerfulness, their graciousness; and I would be the last person on earth to spoil your good time; however, for my few remaining days here, I would appreciate that you keep your talk down to a roar and your whispers down to a shout. Now tell me, what is the problem?

ORSOLA: Tell them to leave my son alone.

CAVALIER: Who has been bothering her son?

ZORZETTO: Him! For no reason, he just started beating me up.

CAVALIER: (*To* ANZOLETTO) Why did you do that?

ANZOLETTO: I don't want him following my girl around. I caught him trying to sneak into her house to bring her a flower.

LUCIETTA: But Gnese, weren't you the one who gave me the flower?

GNESE: Yes. The flower was from me.

CAVALIER: Now you see, it was all a misunderstanding. Come, as before, be friends, be cheerful.

LUCIETTA: You want to come up, Anzoletto?

ANZOLETTO: I don't like this.

CATTE: Get inside, silly. Come on. Come on.

(Takes ANZOLETTO *by the hand and brings him in)*

CAVALIER: She knows how to handle him.

GNESE: He's engaged to her daughter, so you understand.

CAVALIER: Not quite, but I'm learning.

LUCIETTA: *(To* GNESE*)* And you—you should know better. From now on leave him alone.

GNESE: My pleasure.

LUCIETTA: I'm coming, dear one. Here I come!

(Enters her house)

CAVALIER: As it is carnival time after all, I suppose there is nothing really wrong with raising our voices a little. And as I am a stranger here, please allow me to present myself....

ORSOLA: Zorzetto, are you coming in or aren't you?!

ZORZETTO: I'm coming.

ORSOLA: I want to talk to you.

ZORZETTO: Signorina Gnese. *(Bows)*

(Goes inside)

ORSOLA: What do you know: He obeyed me!

(Goes inside)

GNESE: *(Very loud)* Are you coming in, Mamma?

PASQUA: What?

GNESE: Are you coming in?!!!

PASQUA: I'm coming, I want to talk to you.

GNESE: You can talk to me while I work.

CAVALIER: *(To* GNESE*)* My respects. *(Bows)*

GNESE: Sir.

CAVALIER: Goodbye.

GNESE: Here, now, I'll give you a campiello bow.

(She turns her back to him and blows a raspberry. She goes inside.)

CAVALIER: Tell me something. This campiello bow, what precisely does it mean?

PASQUA: What?

CAVALIER: A campiello bow. What does it mean?

PASQUA: Best regards. Here, I'll give it to you too.

(She turns and blows a raspberry.)

CAVALIER: Thank you. I appreciate it. Is the young lady your daughter?

PASQUA: Yes.

CAVALIER: She is well mannered.

PASQUA: Why shouldn't she be? I taught her.

CAVALIER: Does she like to dance?

PASQUA: Come again?

CAVALIER: I say—dancing, does she like it?

PASQUA: What does she dance like? Oh, like a queen. When she dances, people say she looks like lightning.

CAVALIER: I'd love to dance with her.

PASQUA: Oh, yes. Yes. Anytime you want. And me, too, I dance good, too. I taught her.

CAVALIER: Then I would love to dance with you as well.

PASQUA: Oh, yes. Yes. *(To herself)* He's so handsome, I won't dance with anyone but him.

(She goes inside.)

CAVALIER: I am truly indebted to whatever fate brought me here. I wouldn't trade this campiello for a palace. These are my kind of people.

(GASPARINA enters.)

GASPARINA: Let him think what he wants; I'll go to my godmother's, that won't take me long. He probably won't even notice with his head stuck in his books. I've got to get some air.

CAVALIER: *(To himself)* It's her. The one I saw before.

GASPARINA: *(To herself)* It's him. The gentleman.

CAVALIER: *(To himself)* Even lovelier than I remembered. Your servant.

GASPARINA: Sir.

CAVALIER: *(To himself)* Her voice! It's beautiful!

GASPARINA: *(To herself)* I'd better go back.

(Turns to go back inside)

CAVALIER: Have I done something to offend you?

GASPARINA: No, Sir.

CAVALIER: Though it's true that I am a foreigner, I am also a cavalier, so trust that my intentions are honorable.

GASPARINA: *(To herself)* Why do I have this thing for foreigners?

CAVALIER: My wish, if at all possible, is to serve you, and in serving you, you shall see that I serve with honor.

GASPARINA: Sir.

CAVALIER: Let us dispense with ceremony. *Vous avez un mari?*

GASPARINA: *Vous avez* what? Would you mind saying that one more time?

CAVALIER: Have you a husband, my child?

GASPARINA: Oh, a husband! Is that what you're asking me?

CAVALIER: Yes, dear child.

GASPARINA: How could I have a husband when I'm not married?

CAVALIER: That answers my question. And what about your parents? Which ones are they? Have I seen them here this morning?

GASPARINA: I don't think so. My father's dead.

CAVALIER: And your mother?

GASPARINA: Oh, she's dead too.

CAVALIER: Then I probably haven't seen them. So with whom do you live?

GASPARINA: With the whom who is my uncle.

CAVALIER: You live with your uncle? But does not this uncle of yours let you marry?

GASPARINA: I'm still young.

CAVALIER: This is true. Young and very pretty.

GASPARINA: Yes.

CAVALIER: There is a charm about you that intrigues one.

GASPARINA: One what?

CAVALIER: Me.

GASPARINA: Oh. Is this your first time in Venice?

CAVALIER: Yes, my very first time.

GASPARINA: Well, just don't judge it by what you see here. There are people in this town who know how to act proper.

CAVALIER: I have learned this already from you.

GASPARINA: Not to brag, but I know how a lady should stand. Do you see what I mean?

CAVALIER: Oh yes. I see precisely what you mean.

GASPARINA: And when I'm around the people here I talk like them, but when I'm around people there I can talk like them, too.

CAVALIER: Magnificent pronunciation.

GASPARINA: Magnificent what? Where?

CAVALIER: Your speech.

GASPARINA: Oh, my speech. Thank you. Tell me something, have you seen me walk?

CAVALIER: Not enough.

GASPARINA: Here, then, I'll show you. Now watch. Like this. *(Demonstrates)* That's how I used to walk. Like so and so and so. But here's how I walk now. *(Demonstrates)* See? Like so and so and so.

CAVALIER: I like them both.

GASPARINA: I better go to my godmother's now.

CAVALIER: Allow me the pleasure of accompanying you. As your servant.

GASPARINA: I can't, what if my uncle saw?

CAVALIER: But he doesn't have to see, and what he does not see, he does not know.

GASPARINA: No, please. I better go alone.

CAVALIER: If that is your wish. Shall you return soon?

GASPARINA: I'll be back for supper.

CAVALIER: Do not deprive me for long of your charm.

GASPARINA: I won't. I won't.

CAVALIER: Go then. I will keep you no more.

GASPARINA: Sir. *(Curtsies)*

CAVALIER: *Mademoiselle. (Bows)*

GASPARINA: Goodbye.

CAVALIER: *Au revoir.*

GASPARINA: Oh what?

CAVALIER: Goodbye. Goodbye.

GASPARINA: Goodbye. Goodbye.

CAVALIER: Goodbye.

(They leave in opposite directions.)

END OF ACT TWO

ACT THREE

(DONNA CATTE *and* ANZOLETTO *enter from the house.*)

CATTE: Come with me, Son. I want to talk, and I don't want Lucietta to hear.

ANZOLETTO: What's the big secret?

CATTE: That girl in there loves you, and you love her, or why else would you keep coming by? You've already been engaged a year, and that seems long enough to me. And besides, I can't spend the rest of my life chaperoning you two.

ANZOLETTO: So what are you saying?

CATTE: I'm saying, either do it now, or don't hang around so much.

ANZOLETTO: But how can I do it now? I have to get my shop first. Once I get it, I'll marry her.

CATTE: Then stay away until you get it.

ANZOLETTO: I don't like this. You better not be hinting that there's someone else.

CATTE: I'm not hinting anything. Look, Son, I know what it's like. My husband made me wait too. He too couldn't make up his mind, until my mother, I remember what she said, she said: Signor Boldo, either get in or get out.

ANZOLETTO: I'll get in. Just as quick as I can. I promise.

CATTE: But in the meantime, it's best if you stayed away.

ANZOLETTO: Why?!!!

CATTE: I've told you why. I'm tired of being your chaperone.

ANZOLETTO: Is it such a big deal to spend a few hours with us?

CATTE: To be blunt—yes, it is. But there's also another reason, which I can't talk about.

ANZOLETTO: I knew it.

CATTE: You knew what?

ANZOLETTO: There is someone else, isn't there?!

CATTE: You *are* an idiot, aren't you? Now listen to me, dear boy, I'm a widow. I'm old. But that doesn't mean that sometimes, I still don't have...ideas of my own.

ANZOLETTO: Don't make me laugh.

CATTE: So it's funny is it? Well go ahead and laugh at me; you think you know everything. But there's a lot you're not old enough to know.

ANZOLETTO: You want to get married too?

CATTE: I've already made up my mind; soon as the girl's settled.

ANZOLETTO: Now I get it. Dump the girl fast, so you can go off hunting.

CATTE: Put it as crudely as you want, as long as you understand that I don't want you around here until you're ready to marry Lucietta.

ANZOLETTO: Why should she want to marry a peddler?

CATTE: Who cares about what she wants? Think about what you'll get. That girl's been brought up so good you could walk her through an army.

ANZOLETTO: Then what about the dowry you've mentioned?

CATTE: I will try to put it together. I'd let her have her bracelets, her ribbons, a good comfortable bed, with sheets, and four blankets for the children.

ANZOLETTO: Only four? You've got a lot more than four.

CATTE: I need to save something for myself.

ANZOLETTO: Generous, aren't you?

CATTE: Very generous. What else? I'll throw in (Her) two blouses, (Her) three skirts, (Her) one dress and a very nice shawl. What more does she need? And to you, as we've agreed, ten ducats.

ANZOLETTO: You've got the money?

CATTE: Not yet, but I'll get it. Just have to bring her around to two or three houses, and that should pull in at least twenty, maybe more.

ANZOLETTO: You're not going to drag her around like a beggar!

CATTE: Don't be stupid. It's me they'll be giving the money to. I have friends. And they'll see that I'm just trying to make my little girl happy.

ANZOLETTO: *(To himself)* She's not safe with this old woman. I've got to get her away from her.

CATTE: So, Anzoletto, what is it? Yes or no?

ANZOLETTO: It's yes. Yes. I'll marry her this second if you wish.

CATTE: Then she's yours to have. *(Calls)* Lucietta!

LUCIETTA: *(Off)* What is it, Mamma?

ANZOLETTO: Wait. Don't tell her yet.

CATTE: Why not?

ANZOLETTO: I want to surprise her with a ring.

LUCIETTA: *(Coming out)* Were you calling me, Mamma?

CATTE: Congratulations, Lucietta!

LUCIETTA: For what?

ANZOLETTO: *(Quietly, to CATTE)* Shut up! Please!

CATTE: Oh—for nothing.

LUCIETTA: Anzoletto, what's going on?

ANZOLETTO: Oh nothing. Nothing.

CATTE: Look him in the eye.

LUCIETTA: Why? What are you talking about?

CATTE: You'll know yourself this evening.

ANZOLETTO: *(To himself)* You couldn't nail her mouth shut.

LUCIETTA: Come on, tell me.

CATTE: *(To ANZOLETTO)* Should I tell her?

ANZOLETTO: *(To CATTE)* Shut up.

CATTE: But I can't. If I don't tell her I'll choke.

ANZOLETTO: Choke.

LUCIETTA: You've made me very curious.

ANZOLETTO: Go ahead and tell her what the hell you want. I'm going to buy that present.

LUCIETTA: You're leaving?

ANZOLETTO: Yes, but not for long, my pigeon.

(Leaves)

LUCIETTA: So, tell me, Mamma.

CATTE: Oh, be happy, daughter! Be happy! Because when he comes back he's going to marry you!

LUCIETTA: Don't joke, Mama.

CATTE: I fixed everything. What's wrong, don't you want to get married?

LUCIETTA: Do fish want to swim? Do dogs want to bark? Do girls want big bosoms?

CATTE: You've been well graced there, my child.

LUCIETTA: Where did he go?

CATTE: To buy the ring.

LUCIETTA: Really?

CATTE: Really! Really!

LUCIETTA: *(Calls)* Gnese!!!!

CATTE: Sh-sh. You can't tell anyone yet.

GNESE: *(Off)* What is it?

LUCIETTA: Come out. Hurry! Come out!

CATTE: Sh-sh. Not a word.

LUCIETTA: Why?

CATTE: What if he changes his mind?

LUCIETTA: Oh God. He wouldn't dare!

CATTE: Not if he loves you, he wouldn't.

GNESE: *(On her balcony)* What do you want?

CATTE: *(To* LUCIETTA*)* She's here. What are you going to say? Wait! Don't say anything. I'll fix it. I'll fix it. *(To* GNESE*)* We were wondering if you'd like to come down and play sembola?

GNESE: I wish! But I don't think my mamma will let me.

LUCIETTA: Come down!

GNESE: I'll ask my mamma, maybe if she plays too.

(Goes inside)

LUCIETTA: Should I get some boards?

CATTE: Get whatever you want.

LUCIETTA: It'll be nice to sit in the sun.

CATTE: How can you think of playing a game at a time like this?!

LUCIETTA: Why not?

CATTE: Because you are going to get married.

LUCIETTA: I always like to play when I'm happy!

(Goes inside)

CATTE: She's got a lot to learn.

(Goes inside)

(PASQUA and GNESE enter.)

PASQUA: Where'd they go? *(Calls)* Lucietta!!

LUCIETTA: *(Off)* Coming! I'm coming!

GNESE: I'm here whenever you're ready!

PASQUA: *(Very loud)* Where's the bran?

LUCIETTA: *(Off)* Coming!

ZORZETTO: *(From inside)* Hey, if you're playing sembola, I'm playing too!

PASQUA: Yes, yes, you can play too. *(To GNESE)* Come on. Look bright for Zorzetto. Remember what I told you; in a couple of years, he's going to be your husband. *(To ZORZETTO)* Come here. Stay near us.

GNESE: I don't want to look at him.

ZORZETTO: Here I am. Where are we playing?

PASQUA: Has your mother told you?

ZORZETTO: Yes. She's told me. *(To* GNESE*)* Signorina fiancée.

GNESE: *(Smiling)* Silly goose.

*(*LUCIETTA *and* CATTE *bring in the table and bran.)*

LUCIETTA: Here we are. Here we are.

CATTE: *(To herself)* I'll humor her.

LUCIETTA: *(To* ZORZETTO*)* Where's your mamma?

ZORZETTO: Inside.

LUCIETTA: She should play too. *(Calls)* Signora Orsola!!

*(*ORSOLA *enters from her house.)*

ORSOLA: What is it?

LUCIETTA: We're going to play. You want to join us?

ZORZETTO: Come on, Mamma.

ORSOLA: Why not?

PASQUA: Everyone's here.

ORSOLA: Then let's start.

LUCIETTA: A cent each.

PASQUA: *(To* GNESE*)* Go ahead. Say hello.

GNESE: Signora.

ORSOLA: Hello, Gnese. *(To* PASQUA*, in a whisper)* Is she sick?

PASQUA: I told her.

ORSOLA: Oh, she's blushing.

PASQUA: She's happy, but she hides it.

LUCIETTA: *(To* CATTE*)* Mamma, what's going on with Gnese and Zorzetto?

CATTE: I think they're engaged.

LUCIETTA: At her age!

GNESE: Are we playing or not?

LUCIETTA: Ante up. Here's mine.

GNESE: And mine.

ORSOLA: *(To* ZORZETTO*)* Here's two cents. One for you too.

PASQUA: Gnese, can you lend me a penny?

GNESE: Look at her. She never has any money. Here. Take it.

LUCIETTA: Mamma, are you in?

CATTE: Not yet. Not yet. Wait. *(Pulls out a rag)*

ZORZETTO: She hordes her money in a rag.

CATTE: That's so I won't lose it. Here's a penny.

LUCIETTA: So let's play. And no fighting.

ORSOLA: Why would we fight?

LUCIETTA: Stir. Hurry up and stir. *(She stirs the bran.)*

ORSOLA: I want to stir too.

LUCIETTA: Typical. She's never satisfied.

ZORZETTO: Now let me stir it a little.

LUCIETTA: We keep this up, we'll still be stirring tomorrow.

GNESE: Come on. That's enough. Let's make the mounds. *(Puts her hands in the bran)*

LUCIETTA: I want to make the mounds.

(She makes a few mounds with the bran.)

ORSOLA: That's not how you make mounds. Here, I'll show you.

LUCIETTA: No. You'll get oil all over the bran.

ORSOLA: My hands are just as clean, if not cleaner, than yours.

PASQUA: Quit it. I'll make them.

LUCIETTA: Yes, let the oldest do it.

ORSOLA: Yes, the oldest.

PASQUA: Me? You mean Catte, don't you?

CATTE: Old goat.

PASQUA: What? What did you say?

GNESE: Nothing. Nothing.

PASQUA: I didn't hear what you said.

ORSOLA: *(To* ZORZETTO*)* Let's start all over. You make them.

ZORZETTO: If that's all right with everybody. *(Starts to make the mounds)*

GNESE: Just do it. No, that's too small. No, that's too big.

ZORZETTO: You always know better, don't you?

LUCIETTA: Separate them more.

ZORZETTO: There. They're made.

LUCIETTA: I'll take this one.

ORSOLA: That's the one I was going to take.

CATTE: Wait. First we have to settle on the rules.

LUCIETTA: Good idea. That way no one can gripe. Let's go by age.

GNESE: No! Then I'd be last!

LUCIETTA: And I'd be second to last. But do I complain?

PASQUA: Go ahead, Catte. You're first.

CATTE: After you, my dear.

PASQUA: Don't make a fool of yourself.

CATTE: It's you who are making a fool of yourself. I'm at the very least ten years younger.

PASQUA: In your dreams maybe.

LUCIETTA: Wait a minute. Wait. I have another idea. Let's just all grab at the same time.

(Everyone grabs a mound and looks for money)

CATTE: I can't find anything.

GNESE: I got one! And another one! Two more!

LUCIETTA: You got four? *(To* ZORZETTO*)* You fixed it so she'd win, didn't you? He fixed it! He fixed it! I won't accept this.

GNESE: If it means that much to you, here, take them!

LUCIETTA: I will!

CATTE: *(Overlapping)* Take them!

PASQUA, ORSOLA, & ZORZETTO: No don't! Don't! Don't!

*(*FABRIZIO, GASPARINA's *uncle, appears on the balcony with a book in his hand)*

FABRIZIO: What's the meaning of all this noise? Can't you keep it down?!!

LUCIETTA: Oh, I'm sorry. I didn't know we weren't allowed to play in the campiello.

FABRIZIO: Go ahead and play if you want, but that doesn't mean you can upset the whole neighborhood.

LUCIETTA: In the street we can do what we want.

FABRIZIO: I'll have you thrown out of here.

LUCIETTA: Try it. Come on, let's start again.

ORSOLA: Take this, you blowhard!

LUCIETTA: Snotnose!

GNESE: I'll stir the money back in again.

ORSOLA, PASQUA, & ZORZETTO: No, don't! Don't!

FABRIZIO: What insolence! You are trying my patience!

LUCIETTA: (*Singing and dancing in front of* FABRIZIO)
We want to play. We want to play. We want to play.
We want to play.

FABRIZIO: Shut up! I'm warning you: Shut up!

ORSOLA: We want to play. We want to play. We want
to play. We want to play.

FABRIZIO: You don't know what I can do! You'll be
sorry!

ALL: Oh. Oh. We'll be sorry.

(*They laugh loudly.*)

FABRIZIO: Is this how you behave in front of a
gentleman?!!

ALL: Oh. Oh. A gentleman!

(*They laugh.*)

FABRIZIO: They don't know any better.

ALL: "We don't know any better!"

(*All laugh.*)

FABRIZIO: Damn you!!!

(*Throws the book on the table; the bran scatters. He leaves.*)

(All screaming, furiously looking for the money; some of the bran falls on the ground; they look for the money on the ground. They shout, taking the bran from each other's hands.)

(CAVALIER enters from one side, ANZOLETTO from the other.)

(CAVALIER & ANZOLETTO try to calm down the crowd.)

LUCIETTA: I got three!

ORSOLA: Two! Two!

ZORZETTO: One for me!

LUCIETTA: Look how lucky I've been.

GNESE: What about me? I got nothing!

CAVALIER: What's been going on here? What's happened?

LUCIETTA: Oh, nothing. We were just playing a game.

CAVALIER: A game? It sounded like the whole campiello was on fire.

LUCIETTA: Look Anzoletto, three pennies!

ANZOLETTO: Very nice. But aren't you a little old to be playing games in the street?

LUCIETTA: Don't be so serious.

ANZOLETTO: No more. The game's over.

LUCIETTA: Did you bring it?

ANZOLETTO: Bring what?

LUCIETTA: The ring.

ANZOLETTO: You know?

LUCIETTA: I know. Of course, I know.

ANZOLETTO: Then here. Look.

LUCIETTA: Oh, it's beautiful! Mamma, look!

GNESE: *(To* PASQUA*)* What is it?

PASQUA: I can't see.

GNESE: *(Softly)* Signora Orsola, what does he have?

ORSOLA: The ring.

GNESE: No!

ORSOLA: Sh-sh. You'll get one too.

GNESE: When?

ORSOLA: When it's time.

GNESE: When's that?

ORSOLA: When my son marries you.

*(*GNESE *turns, ashamed.)*

PASQUA: *(To* ORSOLA*)* What's wrong with her?

ORSOLA: Blushing again.

PASQUA: Come on, quit that. You don't look good when you blush.

LUCIETTA: Gnese! *(Shows her the ring)*

GNESE: Congratulations.

CAVALIER: May I offer mine as well, and in doing so, join in this happy celebration.

ANZOLETTO: This has nothing to do with you.

CAVALIER: Dear Sir, I am an honest man, and don't intend to spoil your cheerfulness. I have only a good heart and a need for joy.

LUCIETTA: *(To* CATTE*)* Mamma, I have an idea. What if Anzoletto chose him to be best man.

CATTE: Wouldn't that be wonderful! Wait here. Anzoletto?

ANZOLETTO: What?

CATTE: Do you have a best man yet?

ANZOLETTO: No. I hadn't really thought about it.

CATTE: Why don't you pick him.

ANZOLETTO: But I don't even know him.

CATTE: What does that matter? He's just here for the carnival, and once that's over we'll never see him again.

ANZOLETTO: I see what you mean. So once the wedding's over, we won't have the best man hanging around, mooching off us.

CATTE: Should I tell him?

ANZOLETTO: Tell him.

CATTE: *(Quietly, to* LUCIETTA*)* Done! *(To* CAVALIER*)* Sir, I'd like to have a few words with you in private.

CAVALIER: Lead the way, good woman.

(They go aside.)

ANZOLETTO: *(To himself)* She's no dummy, my mother-in-law.

ORSOLA: So Anzoletto, when do you cut the cake?

LUCIETTA: Soon!

ORSOLA: I knew it the moment you walked in.

LUCIETTA: *(To* ANZOLETTO*)* It's true, isn't it?

ORSOLA: Have you picked a date?

LUCIETTA: This evening!

ORSOLA: Oh. *(To herself)* That's good for Catte, she won't have to wait anymore. But me, I've still got two more years of this.

CATTE: Children, this gentleman has agreed to be your best man.

CAVALIER: Yes, and let me add that I am very honored indeed.

ANZOLETTO: Thank you. *(To himself)* I'll be happy when I see the last of him.

CATTE: He's agreed as a favor to me.

GNESE: You must be happy to be getting a ring.

LUCIETTA: What do you say—should we do a "garanghelo"?

ANZOLETTO: Why not? We can tax each other so much per person....

CAVALIER: Excuse me. What does it mean this "garanghelo"?

ANZOLETTO: I'll explain it to you: One person orders a dinner, another person pays, then the person who has paid is paid back by the others in installments of say twenty or thirty cents a month....

ZORZETTO: This way you can have a big dinner without one person paying through the nose.

ORSOLA: I don't know if this is the right sort of occasion for a "garanghelo".

CAVALIER: Excuse me, but what's all this talk of a "garanghelo"? I'm the best man, and I will pay for everything.

LUCIETTA: You mean it?

ORSOLA: He means it.

CATTE: Who invited you, Orsola?

ORSOLA: What do you mean? I better be invited.

CAVALIER: I invite you all!

ORSOLA: Thank you. We'll be there.

GNESE: I don't want to go.

PASQUA: You'll go.

CAVALIER: *(Calls)* Waiter!

(SANSUGA enters.)

SANSUGA: You called?

CAVALIER: Prepare a dinner for everyone. And tell the cook to spare no expense.

SANSUGA: I'll tell him.

LUCIETTA: No, no wait! I want to choose the menu.

CAVALIER: Choose, little bride.

LUCIETTA: Let's see. I want rice with mushrooms, a good hen, and roast veal, and salad, and sweet wine. Now get going. And it better be good because this gentleman's paying.

ORSOLA: I'll bring hot potatoes.

LUCIETTA: Of course.

ORSOLA: The best man can pay me back for them.

SANSUGA: *(To CAVALIER)* Is this the menu you want?

CAVALIER: I leave it up to them.

SANSUGA: It's not a gentleman's sort of meal.

CAVALIER: If I don't care, why should you?

CATTE: Also some round bread.

SANSUGA: Yes, Ma'am.

PASQUA: And lots of minestrone.

ORSOLA: Lots of macaroni.

ANZOLETTO: Salted tongue.

ZORZETTO: At least four slices of roast mutton.

CATTE: And brains. But make sure they're tender.

ORSOLA: You going to remember all this?

SANSUGA: Suddenly there are more side dishes than dinners. *(Leaves)*

(GASPARINA enters.)

GASPARINA: What is this?

CAVALIER: Oh, it's you, Signorina.

LUCIETTA: Did you hear, Gasparina? I got engaged and we're all having dinner together.

CAVALIER: It would please me if you came, too.

GASPARINA: Oh I really couldn't. My uncle, you know, il ne would not approve pas.

LUCIETTA: What did she just say?

GASPARINA: Look at them. How stupid they are. They understand nothing.

CAVALIER: I would gladly, if you would permit me, speak with your uncle and invite him *aussi*.

GASPARINA: Do you wish to come upstairs?

CAVALIER: May I, *Mademoiselle?*

GASPARINA: *Oui*, Sir *Monsieur*.

LUCIETTA: Listen to her!

ORSOLA: Shameless.

GASPARINA: *(To the others)* Don't tell me you don't understand French?

LUCIETTA: *(Affected)* All you know is "*oui*".

GASPARINA: Listen to them, Sir *Monsieur*. Please excuse me, but I fear they would not be suitable company for a lady.

CAVALIER: Your absence would cause me great sadness.

LUCIETTA: *(To* ORSOLA*)* Let's get her to come. That'll be worth a few laughs.

ORSOLA: *(To* LUCIETTA*)* Yes. Yes. *(To* GASPARINA*)* Gasparina, you are right, we aren't worthy to eat with you, but couldn't you come anyway?

GASPARINA: If I could, I would, but I can't come alone.

LUCIETTA: Come on, we'll let you sit at the head.

GASPARINA: Thank you. And if I did come, the head is where I would expect to sit, but I cannot come without my uncle, *Mademoiselle.*

ORSOLA: Gnese, you tell her to come.

GNESE: Come on, we're all going.

GASPARINA: A single girl belongs in the house.

CAVALIER: I'm afraid we are not getting anywhere.

GASPARINA: Tell me, do you know what pronunciation is?

GNESE: No, what's that?

GASPARINA: Pity. You explain it to her, Sir *Monsieur.* *(*FABRIZIO *enters on the balcony.)* It's my uncle!

CAVALIER: Your servant, Sir.

FABRIZIO: What's going on down there?

GASPARINA: Uncle, be quiet. Don't embarrass me!

FABRIZIO: Get inside. Now!

CAVALIER: Sir, I would not jump to any conclusions. Your niece has done nothing improper.

FABRIZIO: *(To* GASPARINA*)* Don't make me say it again!

GASPARINA: *(To* CAVALIER*)* Your humble servant.

FABRIZIO: Go!!!

GASPARINA: *(To* CAVALIER*)* I'm sorry.

CAVALIER: Not as sorry as I am.

GASPARINA: *(Curtsies)* I am your servant.

FABRIZIO: Not another word!

CAVALIER: *Mademoiselle.*

GASPARINA: Sir, *Monsieur.*

(She enters the house.)

FABRIZIO: I now see the kind of man you are.

CAVALIER: You wrong me, Sir.

FABRIZIO: No, you wrong her. You and these insolent women!!

LUCIETTA: What did we do?

ORSOLA: Don't you insult us!

ALL: Now you listen to us, big mouth!

FABRIZIO: I'll listen to nothing.

(Goes inside)

(All laugh.)

CAVALIER: I don't know what to do. Let us go and dine. I will try to see her later, but in the meantime, let us eat.

(Goes into the inn)

ORSOLA: Zorzetto, take Gnese's arm.

GNESE: I don't need any help, thank you.

(She enters the inn.)

ZORZETTO: Why does she act like that?

ORSOLA: She'll change. She'll change.

(They go into the inn.)

PASQUA: Glad I didn't eat much for breakfast.

(Enters the inn)

CATTE: Come on, children, let's go. *(To herself)* Wish it was me getting married. *(Enters the inn)*

ANZOLETTO: All right, let's go in and do it up right. But after this, there'll be no more parties or inns.

(Enters the inn)

LUCIETTA: Anzoletto, wait for me! *(To herself)* I'm so excited. I feel like my heart's going to burst through my side. I'll eat myself sick, 'cause I'm the bride!

(Enters the inn)

END OF ACT THREE

ACT FOUR

(CAVALIER *comes out of the inn. He no longer has his hat or sword.*)

CAVALIER: Enough. Enough. I can't take it anymore. Though I must admit I have never had such a good time. But still I can't take it anymore. My head hurts. The noise. Those endless ridiculous toasts. Sober, they're not. I need some air; and while I'm out here I can talk to that uncle of Gasparina's, and get him to account for his insulting behavior. Though this time he better watch what he says; I feel a little hot headed at the moment, and it wouldn't take much to provoke me. Hey you in there! (GASPARINA *enters on her balcony.*) Madame.

GASPARINA: What do you want? Go away, quick!

CAVALIER: I came to see your uncle.

GASPARINA: Please, for my sake, go!

CAVALIER: What has happened?

GASPARINA: He said to me. He said.... Oh, I cannot say it!

CAVALIER: Tell your uncle to come down here.

GASPARINA: He said to me....

CAVALIER: You need not repeat his insults. Allow me to deal with him. Go!

GASPARINA: I will go then. I am going. *(Starts to withdraw, then turns back)* Wait. This much I can tell you. He said to me a bad word.

CAVALIER: What bad word?

GASPARINA: I don't want him to see me. I must go.

(Starts to withdraw, stops, turns back)

CAVALIER: Yes. Go.

GASPARINA: Wait. This is what he said to me. He said: You are a dumb bunny. "Dumb bunny." Do you think he was trying to say I'm stupid?

CAVALIER: I think so. Yes. Now quick, go, before he sees you.

GASPARINA: Stupid?! Well he has his nerve. Of all people to call stupid! If I'm so stupid then how come I can speak French? I'd like to see him find another girl in this town who reads as much as I read. When I go to a comedy at the theater, just as soon as it is over, I can tell you if it was good or bad. Just as soon as it is over! And when I say it is bad, I am always right! Does that sound stupid to you?!

CAVALIER: Madame, your uncle!

GASPARINA: That's not to say there aren't stupid girls around; but I'm not like them. I like to study. I like to learn things. Did you know that I can repeat, almost word for word, a story, even if I have only read it once!

(FABRIZIO enters from the house. He greets the CAVALIER without speaking.)

CAVALIER: *(To FABRIZIO)* Your servant.

GASPARINA: *(Thinking she is the one being greeted)* Are you leaving? But I'm not finished.

FABRIZIO: *(To* GASPARINA; *coming into her line of sight)* Yes you are.

GASPARINA: Oh God! Oh God!

(Goes inside)

FABRIZIO: Sir, your ability to annoy seems to me to be a bit excessive.

CAVALIER: I came to see you.

FABRIZIO: What do you want from me?

CAVALIER: One of my rank is usually afforded more courtesy.

FABRIZIO: I do not know you and I know nothing about you, but you must know that an uncle's honor demands that he protect his ward.

CAVALIER: I have done nothing that would require your protection; and besides, she is not exactly nobility.

FABRIZIO: You do not know who she is.

CAVALIER: I know what I've learned, and that is that her father was a shopkeeper and her family poor.

FABRIZIO: Her father, my brother, fled Naples because of a duel of honor, and on arriving in Venice was forced to learn a trade. Sadly he married a woman beneath him. So it is true that he was poor in life, but at birth he was a nobleman.

CAVALIER: From Naples?

FABRIZIO: Yes.

CAVALIER: I too am from Naples. Perhaps you know my name. I am the Cavalier Astolfi.

FABRIZIO: Then I beg your pardon. Your father was known and much admired by me.

CAVALIER: Then you must know that he died.

FABRIZIO: I have heard, yes; as I have heard—if I may be blunt—that his son has frittered away his fortune.

CAVALIER: True. After years of wandering this world, my purse is nearly empty.

FABRIZIO: What do you think you will do?

CAVALIER: I do not know. Everything I own is mortgaged.

FABRIZIO: Sir, allow me to suggest, that this is not the way to live.

CAVALIER: Let us not talk about such things now. I have enough for these four days of the carnival.

FABRIZIO: And then what?

CAVALIER: We shall see. But what is to be, is to be. What is your name? Do I know you?

FABRIZIO: Fabrizio Dei Ritorti.

CAVALIER: Wait. Are you the Fabrizio who, being reduced to the deepest poverty, gained a fortune back by winning the lottery?

FABRIZIO: Not a fortune; but enough to keep me comfortable.

CAVALIER: We should all live to be so comfortable.

FABRIZIO: Part of what I won must be kept as a dowry for my niece.

CAVALIER: How much would that be?

FABRIZIO: It will depend upon the match.

CAVALIER: Does she know this?

FABRIZIO: She knows nothing. I have wanted first to watch her and examine her, though soon it will be time to see her married.

CAVALIER: *(To himself)* I think I'm in love.

FABRIZIO: *(To himself)* I would let her have three or four thousand scudi, even more if necessary, to see her set up well.

CAVALIER: Have you a husband in mind?

FABRIZIO: No. The opportunities have not as yet presented themselves.

*(*LUCIETTA, ANZOLETTO, CATTE, PASQUA, ORSOLA, GNESE, *and* ZORZETTO *enter onto the balcony of the inn.)*

LUCIETTA: Hey you, Cavalier! To your health!

(She drinks.)

CAVALIER: I'm honored!

FABRIZIO: *(To* CAVALIER*)* If you would excuse me, Sir.

CAVALIER: Where are you going?

FABRIZIO: To get away from these possessed women.

(He goes into his house.)

LUCIETTA: Where's he going? He's not coming up?

CATTE: I'm stuffed.

CAVALIER: Strength, friends! Drink and be happy!

PASQUA: Come on, let's drink!

LUCIETTA: *(With a glass in her hand)* To the Sir Monsieur!

CAVALIER: Thank you! Drink, happy people!

PASQUA: To the health of the one who's paying the bill!

(All cheer.)

LUCIETTA: Quiet, I'm going to make a beautiful toast that rhymes.

"When I am happy, bad words I do not say,
To the health of my handsome fiancé!"

(All cheer.)

ORSOLA: Me too. Me too. Fill it. Come on, fill it!
(Holds up her glass)

ANZOLETTO: You've got some wine in there.
(Pours her more wine)

ORSOLA: "With this drop of wine,
that's sweet and red,
I make my toast, in rhyme,
to the fathead!"

(All cheer.)

LUCIETTA: Who do you mean?

ORSOLA: Don't be stupid. Don't you know?

(Indicates the CAVALIER*)*

CAVALIER: Very good. Nothing like laughing while
you drink. Now it's my turn.

ANZOLETTO: First me! First me!
"Toast you I will every day of the year,
As long as you stay far away from here."

CAVALIER: "My reply to you, let me put it like this,
Life away from you, is my word for bliss."

(All cheer.)

PASQUA: Ready?!! *(To* ANZOLETTO*)* Give me a drink.

ANZOLETTO: Take, old woman.

PASQUA: Who are you calling an old woman, you
little pup?!
"And even if I were old, I'd still be a good catch,
To the health and happiness of this fine match!"

(All cheer.)

CATTE: Hurry! Give me! Give me! *(Gets a drink)*
"To be without a husband, I can hardly stand it,
To these fine young people, I got to hand it."

(All cheer.)

ZORZETTO: I want to make one too! Can I?

ORSOLA: Do it. Do it.

ZORZETTO: *(To* ANZOLETTO*)* Come on, will you give
me some wine?!! *(Gets some wine)*
"With this nice wine that I now twirl,
I toast the health of my nice girl."

(All cheer)

PASQUA: Gnese, you too. Show them how smart you
are.

ORSOLA: Answer him.

GNESE: *(To* ANZOLETTO*)* Give me something to drink.

ORSOLA: Speak from your heart.

ZORZETTO: *(Grabs the bottle from* ANZOLETTO*)* I'll give
it to her.

ANZOLETTO: Don't be so grabby.

ZORZETTO: Mind your own business!

LUCIETTA: Shut your mouth, piss pot.

GNESE: "With this wine, that from the grape did flow,
I drink to the health...."

PASQUA: Of Zorzetto!

GNESE: No, of Anzoletto.

ZORZETTO: Who???

LUCIETTA: *(To* GNESE*)* You sneaky little bitch! I'll slap
your face in!

ORSOLA: Stop it! Stop it!

PASQUA: We'll see whose face gets slapped!

CATTE: You ugly old woman!

ORSOLA: Stop it!

LUCIETTA: Try it, hot potato peddler!!!

ALL: *(Shout and yell as they go inside)* What? Shut up!
You shut up! You heard what I said! Come here! Get
inside! *(Etc.)*

CAVALIER: *(Alone)* One second they are toasting, then
the next, they're screaming. Must be the wine. I better
go settle them down. I will get them to see reason;
if not with words, then with a stick.

(Enters the inn)

(GASPARINA enters on her balcony.)

GASPARINA: What's all the noise? It sounded like the
devil himself was out here.

FABRIZIO: *(Has entered)* They do it to spite me. I can't
take it anymore.

GASPARINA: Uncle, where are you going?

FABRIZIO: To find another house. I don't care if it's
a gutted basement, just as long as it's far away from
them.

GASPARINA: Yes. All their fighting it does wear on one.

FABRIZIO: I am surprised that Cavalier Astolfi
encourages such people.

GASPARINA: Who?

FABRIZIO: You know who I mean.

GASPARINA: Is that his name? Do you know him?

FABRIZIO: I knew his noble family, whose fortune he
has done his best to ruin.

GASPARINA: Uncle, can we talk?

FABRIZIO: In the street? Have you no sense of propriety? We shall talk later, first I must find us a new house. *(Takes a few steps)* Have my snuff box sent down, will you?

GASPARINA: Yes, Sir.

(Goes inside)

FABRIZIO: I feel like my nerves have been stripped bare. Normal everyday noise, well that I can take; but this, it is pure madness, and it is me who's being driven mad.

(GASPARINA enters from the house with his snuff box.)

GASPARINA: Here it is.

FABRIZIO: I didn't tell *you* to bring it down!

GASPARINA: You know your servant's ill.

FABRIZIO: Then you should have thrown it down. I have told you before, I do not want you out here in the street!

(Takes snuff box)

GASPARINA: I won't do it again.

FABRIZIO: You behave as common as your mother. Your father should be cursed for forgetting his blood.

GASPARINA: Are we noble, Uncle?

FABRIZIO: Go!

GASPARINA: It's just that at times, I feel like I must be!

FABRIZIO: I said—get inside! I don't want you out here anymore!

GASPARINA: You don't have to shout.

(Goes inside)

FABRIZIO: As long as she's still with me, I will never get any studying done. Be best to marry her off the first chance I get.

(Leaves)

*(*CAVALIER *enters, followed by* SANSUGA.*)*

CAVALIER: We got them settled down.

SANSUGA: The only way to deal with those kind of people is with the back of your hand. You were too soft with them.

CAVALIER: Let us say that I find them amusing. They shall be out soon set to sing and dance, and that will give me pleasure. I enjoy watching people dance, and I expect I shall dance a little myself.

SANSUGA: You want the bill?

CAVALIER: Let me see it. Seventy lira! Don't be ridiculous!

SANSUGA: It was thirty just for the wine.

CAVALIER: I'll pay you sixty-five. No more.

SANSUGA: I wouldn't want you to be unhappy.

CAVALIER: Here. Take it.

SANSUGA: And then there's my tip.

CAVALIER: Here's five lira. You'll get no more.

SANSUGA: Thank you, Sir.

CAVALIER: I'm sorry to drive such a hard bargain, but what's fair is fair.

SANSUGA: Yes. What's fair is fair.

CAVALIER: Tell them they can come out now.

(Noise off)

SANSUGA: I think they don't have to be told.

(SANSUGA *leaves.*)

CAVALIER: If I make it through this carnival with a cent left, it will be a miracle. That dowry could solve my problems, if Fabrizio would let me have his niece. And after all, she does have some noble blood; so what if her mother was from another class, my mother was our chambermaid.

GASPARINA: *(On her balcony)* Cavalier Astolfi!

CAVALIER: Oh my dear lady, what I had only guessed, I now know as the truth. Let me give you my heart, one noble to another.

(GASPARINA *curtsies.*)

CAVALIER: Your uncle has told me everything. We are both of the same town. We are both of the same world. We are both of the same rank—sort of.

GASPARINA: I know.

CAVALIER: He would like to see you married.

GASPARINA: Yes?

CAVALIER: I pray to Heaven that I could be the fortunate one.

GASPARINA: Tell me: Do people call you "your excellence"?

CAVALIER: In some places. Yes.

GASPARINA: Then they would call me "your lady excellence." But I think that's too long, don't you?

CAVALIER: You want a title? We'll find you a title.

GASPARINA: Really?!!!! *(Noise from the inn)* What's that noise?

CAVALIER: My friends are coming.

GASPARINA: Then I must go. Such company is not suitable for me anymore.

CAVALIER: Your servant.

GASPARINA: Goodbye.

(She goes. CATTE, PASQUA, ANZOLETTO, LUCIETTA, ORSOLA, GNESE, and ZORZETTO enter. With them are other people who enter playing instruments. All enter dancing or playing.)

LUCIETTA: I can't anymore. Come with me, Anzoletto.

CATTE: I have to lie down.

(Goes inside her house)

ANZOLETTO: *(To LUCIETTA)* Tired? The way you dance I'm not surprised.

LUCIETTA: What's wrong with you? Can't a girl have some fun? A bride's supposed to enjoy herself.

(Goes into her house)

ANZOLETTO: She won't dance like that, when I'm her husband.

(Follows LUCIETTA)

PASQUA: I can't see! I can't see! My eyes!

GNESE: Come with me.

PASQUA: Give me your hand; I don't want to fall down.

GNESE: Let's go. Come on.

(Leads her by the hand)

ZORZETTO: *(To GNESE)* You don't say goodbye?

GNESE: *(To ZORZETTO)* You silly boy.

(They leave.)

ORSOLA: Boy. Come here. Don't worry, give her time. It's obvious she's crazy about you.

(Enters her house)

ZORZETTO: Yes. But I wish I didn't have to wait two years.

(Enters his house)

CAVALIER: Not even a thank you.

(Enters the inn)

END OF ACT FOUR

ACT FIVE

(FABRIZIO *enters with four* PORTERS. GASPARINA *is on her balcony.*)

FABRIZIO: *(To* PORTERS*)* Come on. Come on. Shake a leg I want to get this over with.

GASPARINA: Uncle, who are these men?

FABRIZIO: Porters. I found a house. We can be moved in by evening.

GASPARINA: Moved? So soon?

FABRIZIO: The sooner the better. *(To* PORTERS*)* Come with me.

GASPARINA: Wait. Do we have to? What if I don't like it?

FABRIZIO: You'll like it.

GASPARINA: Is it big?

FABRIZIO: Big enough.

GASPARINA: It is by the water? Will we have a gondola?

FABRIZIO: What do you want a gondola for?

GASPARINA: Just a tiny gondola. Either we get a gondola or I'm not going.

FABRIZIO: I'm getting very tired of you. *(To* PORTERS*)* Let's go.

(CAVALIER enters.)

CAVALIER: Fabrizio, can I have a word with you?

FABRIZIO: *(To himself)* I'm getting tired of him, too.
(To CAVALIER) What do you want?

CAVALIER: *(Seems to greet FABRIZIO, but in fact is greeting GASPARINA)* Your servant.

FABRIZIO: What is it?

CAVALIER: Your servant, Sir.

FABRIZIO: *(Noticing GASPARINA)* Oh. I see.
(To PORTERS) You go in the house. *(To GASPARINA)*
And you: Do the same, and start packing.

GASPARINA: *(To herself)* If only I'd get married!

FABRIZIO: *(To himself)* Let's hope there's something in
this.

GASPARINA: *(To herself)* I'd even settle for just a little
bitty title. *(Goes inside)*

FABRIZIO: What is it? I'm in a hurry.

CAVALIER: Then I shall be blunt. Sir, your niece has
wounded my heart.

FABRIZIO: Is it your heart or your purse that you are
worried about?

CAVALIER: Her virtue has awakened my deepest
affections.

FABRIZIO: *(To himself)* I'm of half a mind to give her to
him, just to be rid of her.

CAVALIER: You know who I am.

FABRIZIO: Yes. And I know the way you have been
living your life, and if I were you I wouldn't be too
proud of that.

CAVALIER: I am not. And I plan to change. In the future I shall live moderately, and in time return to my town and live prudently.

FABRIZIO: Why should I believe you?

CAVALIER: I swear it to you as an honorable cavalier.

FABRIZIO: But first you would have to get out of your present financial mess. How do you propose to achieve that?

CAVALIER: How much is her dowry?

FABRIZIO: Then it's as I thought. How do I know you won't spend that as well?

CAVALIER: Then insure the dowry against my possessions.

FABRIZIO: I thought everything was mortgaged.

CAVALIER: You could redeem them, and I could sign over to you everything for, say, ten years, longer if you wish. I shall depend only upon you, and upon your love and advice, and shall mature under your guidance as if I were your son.

FABRIZIO: Enough. I have to think about it.

CAVALIER: Please, don't keep me in suspense.

FABRIZIO: You want an answer in the middle of the street?

CAVALIER: Let's go inside.

FABRIZIO: Let's talk tomorrow.

CAVALIER: I am prepared to renounce my former life now, here, why should you make me wait?

FABRIZIO: But we haven't finished talking!!

CAVALIER: So let's talk.

FABRIZIO: *(To himself)* I can't decide.

CAVALIER: I beg you.

FABRIZIO: Let's go.

CAVALIER: *(To himself)* It's my last hope.

(Enters the house)

FABRIZIO: *(To himself)* If he means it, he's got her.

(Goes inside)

*(*LUCIETTA *enters on her balcony.)*

LUCIETTA: *(Seeing the* CAVALIER *enter* GASPARINA's *house)* Oh my God. They got him inside! *(Calling)* Gnese! Gnese!

GNESE: Who's calling me?

LUCIETTA: Me! Me! Your best friend!

GNESE: What is it?

LUCIETTA: He went in. There! *(Points to* GASPARINA's *house)*

GNESE: No!

LUCIETTA: Yes! I swear! Cross my heart and hope to die! *(Calls)* Orsola! ·

ORSOLA: What do you want?

LUCIETTA: Listen. The foreigner, he went into Gasparina's house. She literally dragged him in.

ORSOLA: That flirt!

LUCIETTA: She's a dirty penny, all right.

ORSOLA: Where's her uncle?

LUCIETTA: He's in there too!

ORSOLA: *(To* GNESE) Go call your mother, she should know about this.

GNESE: No, I don't want to.

LUCIETTA: What's wrong? Is she sick?

GNESE: She's sleeping.

LUCIETTA: Still?!

GNESE: The wine didn't agree with her. She threw up.

ORSOLA: Old women should know better.

LUCIETTA: My mother's just as bad. She's already fallen down four times.

GNESE: Where is she?

LUCIETTA: On the bed, snoring.

ORSOLA: Where's Anzoletto?

LUCIETTA: He fell asleep in the fireplace.

GNESE: In the fireplace?!

ORSOLA: When are you two getting married?

LUCIETTA: Anytime now.

ORSOLA: And the best man?

LUCIETTA: He said—He'll come when we call him.

ORSOLA: Best of luck to both of you.

LUCIETTA: And to you.

ORSOLA: Just two years to go, right, Gnese?

GNESE: What?

LUCIETTA: Why are you always blushing? He's not so bad as all that.

ORSOLA: *(To* LUCIETTA*)* Come here, I'll fill you in.

GNESE: *(To* ORSOLA*)* Do you have to tell her everything?!

ORSOLA: What's the big secret? Why shouldn't she know? Lucietta, are you coming?

LUCIETTA: What else is there to do with everybody asleep?

ORSOLA: Good girl, hurry. Come on.

GNESE: Signora Orsola....

ORSOLA: Why don't you call me Mamma?

GNESE: *(Covers her face)* Oh!

ORSOLA: Child, I am getting sick and tired of all your whining!

GNESE: If you yell at me, I'll never speak to you again.

ORSOLA: Daughter...

LUCIETTA: I'm coming. I'm coming.

(Comes running out, toward ORSOLA's *house)*

ORSOLA: Come upstairs.

(Goes inside)

LUCIETTA: *(To* GNESE*)* Two years isn't that long. Though I'll bet you'd give anything to be in my shoes right now!

(Goes inside)

GNESE: She makes me so mad! I'll take Zorzetto. But does the whole world have to know it!

*(*PORTERS *return from* GASPARINA's *house, with household goods.)*

GNESE: Are they moving? That's what it looks like. And if they move out, then we could move in. *(Calls)* Mamma! I don't want to stay in this little house anymore! And when I get married...but that's not for a while yet. There's so much to look forward to!

*(*ANZOLETTO *enters.)*

ANZOLETTO: Gnese, have you seen Lucietta?

GNESE: She's in with Signora Orsola.

ANZOLETTO: Wonderful! She knows I don't want her going in there. And yet she goes! I'll make her pay for this! Why can't that old woman leave her alone?! I'll slap her silly, that's what I'll do. But first, I'll talk to her mother. Hey Catte! Donna Catte! Wake up!

(Knocks hard)

CATTE: Who's knocking?

ANZOLETTO: Come downstairs, I want to talk to you.

GNESE: Oh my God! He's going to start beating her before they're married!

CATTE: Is that my son-in-law?

ANZOLETTO: What the hell are you doing? Passed out like a dead sack while your daughter—

CATTE: Where is she?

ANZOLETTO: She's wandered off.

CATTE: Wandered off??!!

ANZOLETTO: To the potato peddler's. There.

CATTE: Oh. What's wrong with that? Let her stay.

ANZOLETTO: I don't want her to go there!

CATTE: Why? Don't tell me you're jealous of her son? Of that skinny ugly little boy?

GNESE: Who's ugly?!!

CATTE: Come on, don't be stupid. Look, here she comes now.

(LUCIETTA enters.)

LUCIETTA: You finally woke up. *(To ANZOLETTO)* What's the matter with you? You look like you're angry or something.

ANZOLETTO: Flirt!

(Slaps her)

LUCIETTA: *(Crying)* What did you do that for?!!!

CATTE: You're crazy. You don't deserve to marry my daughter!

ANZOLETTO: Who'd want to marry her?!

CATTE: *(Crying)* Don't worry, my child. There. There. We'll get you another husband.

ANZOLETTO: *(To* LUCIETTA*)* Give me my ring back.

LUCIETTA: *(Crying)* Never!

CATTE: You want it back? I'll get it back!

(Goes to remove the ring from LUCIETTA*)*

LUCIETTA: *(Crying)* Mamma, leave me alone!

CATTE: Don't holler at me! Give me the ring!

LUCIETTA: You'd have to kill me first!

CATTE: He treats you like this and you still want him?!

LUCIETTA: *(Crying)* I want him! Yes!!!!

CATTE: Then you deserve him. But don't come crying to me if he kills you!!!

ANZOLETTO: *(Sobbing)* Listen. You know why I slapped you? Because I love you.

LUCIETTA: I know.

CATTE: Scum. Bastard.

LUCIETTA: I don't care what he is, I want him!

CATTE: Pathetic!

ANZOLETTO: Signora, Mother-in-law, can't you understand? You're a woman.

GNESE: *(To herself)* I'd be afraid to marry him if I were her.

CATTE: How can you treat my child like this?!

ANZOLETTO: *(To* LUCIETTA*)* Come on, let's go. Aren't you coming?

LUCIETTA: Bastard. Do you love me?

CATTE: Let's get off the street.

ANZOLETTO: It's all because of that asshole, Zorzetto.

GNESE: Don't you talk about him like that!!!

ANZOLETTO: Go tell him what I called him!

LUCIETTA: Come on, silly. Don't start anything.

CATTE: You shouldn't talk like that.

ANZOLETTO: Go to hell!

CATTE: Shut your mouth!

LUCIETTA: Let's go. Let's go.

CATTE: Come on. Quick. Inside.

LUCIETTA: You won't hit me anymore, will you?

ANZOLETTO: Not unless you make me.

LUCIETTA: I won't make you. I promise.

(Enters the house)

CATTE: Poor child. Already he's started to beat her up.

(Enters the house)

GNESE: He might knock some sense into her. *(Calls)* Signora Orsola!

ORSOLA: *(On her balcony)* What is it?

*(*ZORZETTO *enters downstairs.)*

GNESE: Did you hear what happened?

ORSOLA: No, what happened?

GNESE: Anzoletto was looking for Lucietta, and when he found out she was with you he started yelling, then when she came out, he hit her in the face.

ORSOLA: No?! Really? I'm not surprised. What's wrong with her coming here? What does he think she was doing?

GNESE: He thought she was doing something all right, because he blamed Zorzetto and called him an asshole.

ZORZETTO: An asshole?

ORSOLA: Sh-sh. Not so loud. Come inside.

ZORZETTO: He can't call me that and get away with it.

GNESE: Wait. Don't start anything. I think he's crazy.

ORSOLA: Come inside, Son.

ZORZETTO: I'm coming. *(To himself)* I'll get him. I'll get him.

(Goes inside)

ORSOLA: Why did you have to tell me this? You trying to start a fight?

GNESE: I thought you'd want to know.

ORSOLA: Use your head!

GNESE: I'm sorry. Wait, I'll get my mamma, she'll make things better.

(Goes inside, as does ORSOLA*)*

*(*ZORZETTO *returns with some stones.)*

ZORZETTO: He calls me an asshole. He'll get his.

(Throws some stones at LUCIETTA's *balcony)*

CATTE: *(On her balcony)* Who's doing that?

ZORZETTO: Stupid old woman, catch this! *(Throws a stone at her)*

CATTE: Help! *(Holds her head)* He hit me! He hit me! *(Goes inside)*

ORSOLA: *(Returning)* What happened? What are you doing?

ZORZETTO: Nothing, Mamma.

ORSOLA: I told you to come inside. Now come!

(ANZOLETTO enters from the house with a big knife.)

ANZOLETTO: Come here, shit face.

ORSOLA: *(Shouting from the balcony)* My son! My son!

(ZORZETTO runs into the house.)

ANZOLETTO: Come out here, punk!

LUCIETTA: *(On her balcony)* What are you doing?

GNESE: *(On her balcony)* Fight! Fight! Fight!

ANZOLETTO: Scum. Both of them. Mother and son.

ORSOLA: *(From her balcony, throws a vase)* Scum are we!!!

LUCIETTA & GNESE: Help!!!!!!!

ANZOLETTO: Come out here, unless you're too chicken! *(He goes back inside.)*

ZORZETTO: *(Enters with a cane)* Who's chicken?!!!

LUCIETTA: He's got a cane!!!

(SANSUGA enters from the inn, armed.)

SANSUGA: What's happening?!! Stop this!

LUCIETTA: Help!! *(Goes inside)*

GNESE: Help!

CAVALIER: *(Entering on the balcony)* What's all the noise?

GNESE: Sir *Monsieur*, go down there quick. Stop it! Stop it! *(He goes inside.)*

ANZOLETTO: *(Returning)* I'll kill you.

ZORZETTO: Stay back!

SANSUGA: Someone's going to get hurt!!!!

ORSOLA: *(Entering with a frying pan)* My son! My son!

LUCIETTA: *(Entering, pulling* ANZOLETTO *away)* Come with me!

ORSOLA: *(Pulling* ZORZETTO*)* Get inside! *(Takes away his cane)* Give me that cane!

LUCIETTA: *(Pulling* ANZOLETTO*)* If you love me, come!!

ANZOLETTO: *(Looks at* ZORZETTO*)* You're right. Why waste my time. *(Goes inside with* LUCIETTA*)*

ORSOLA: *(To* SANSUGA*)* Put that gun away.

SANSUGA: You people never change. *(Goes inside the inn)*

ORSOLA: *(To* ZORZETTO*)* Now get your butt inside. I don't want to have to tell you again.

ZORZETTO: But he called me an asshole. *(Goes inside)*

ORSOLA: Just like his father—the brains of a bird. Lucky for him he has me. *(She goes inside.)*

PASQUA: *(Enters from her house)* Calling that child names, he ought to be ashamed of himself. At last he's shown his true self.

CATTE: Him? What about the other one? He was throwing rocks at me!

PASQUA: He was just getting even.

CATTE: Why are you taking his side? Get out of here, or it's me who'll be getting even.

PASQUA: Oh what a face! "I'm scared." "I'm scared." *(Laughs)*

CATTE: Keep that up and I'll pull out your hair.

PASQUA: Too bad I can't do the same to you, but you don't have any to pull!

CATTE: You're the one who's deaf.

PASQUA: But I have teeth.

CATTE: Old rag!

PASQUA: Turd!

CATTE: You want to "play"?

PASQUA: Yes. Let's "play." *(They fight.)*

CATTE: *(Calls)* Lucietta!!!

PASQUA: *(Calls)* Daughter!!!

(LUCIETTA, GNESE, and ORSOLA all enter onto the street.)

LUCIETTA: Mamma!

GNESE: Stop it!

ORSOLA: Quit this!

ANZOLETTO: *(Entering with knife)* Leave my mother-in-law alone!

ZORZETTO: *(Entering with cane)* What did you say?!

LUCIETTA, GNESE, & ORSOLA: Help!!!!!!!!!!!!!

(CAVALIER enters.)

CAVALIER: Don't you ever get tired of this?!!!! Shut up! Or I'll beat the hell out of all of you!

LUCIETTA: They were beating up my mamma!

PASQUA: *(Pointing to CATTE)* It's her fault!

ORSOLA: I tried to stop them.

CAVALIER: Quiet!!!! Enough is enough. And on all days, to pick a wedding day! Where are your manners?!!! *(To* ANZOLETTO*)* Put that knife down.

LUCIETTA: Give it to me. *(Takes the knife)* I don't know what you planned to do with this thing. *(Takes it inside. Returns later.)*

CAVALIER: *(To* ZORZETTO*)* And that cane. Put it away.

ORSOLA: Yes, Sir.

(Takes the cane from ZORZETTO*)*

CAVALIER: Pitiful. That's what you all are. Have you nothing better to do than scream at each other?!!

LUCIETTA: I didn't scream at anyone.

ORSOLA: I never did open my mouth.

CATTE: I never heard my daughter say a word.

PASQUA: Right. She's so quiet she could pass for a mute.

LUCIETTA: Now wait a minute....

GNESE: It's you who should wait a minute....

LUCIETTA: Why? You got something to say to me?

CAVALIER: Please, no more of this. I am leaving tomorrow and if you all can contain yourself until this evening, I would like to invite you to dinner.

CATTE: Oh. Actually, I was never really upset.

PASQUA: What did he say?

ORSOLA: Didn't you hear him? He said if we're nice he'll invite us to dinner.

PASQUA: Oh. Who hasn't been nice?

CAVALIER: The older you get the shorter the memory.

ORSOLA: Lucietta, have I done anything to offend you?

LUCIETTA: Nothing, my good friend.

ORSOLA: Let me give you a kiss.

(Kisses her)

LUCIETTA: Let me give one to you. *(Kisses her)* What do you have to say for yourself, Gnese?

GNESE: Me, I keep my mouth shut.

PASQUA: Catte....

CATTE: Pasqua....

PASQUA & CATTE: Give us a kiss.

(Kiss each other)

CAVALIER: *(To* ZORZETTO *and* ANZOLETTO*)* And what about you, boys? Don't you want to shake hands?

ORSOLA: Go on, Zorzetto. Stick out your hand.

ANZOLETTO: Is this necessary?

LUCIETTA: If you love me, shake his hand.

ANZOLETTO: All right.

(They shake hands.)

CAVALIER: Now that peace has been victorious, we shall all be able to dine together. Now let me tell you my news—I too have become a bridegroom. This evening, I shall marry.

LUCIETTA: Marry who?

*(*GASPARINA *enters on her balcony.)*

GASPARINA: Me.

LUCIETTA: What do you know....

ORSOLA: Congratulations.

GNESE: How did this happen?

LUCIETTA: Come down, so I can give you a kiss.

CAVALIER: Come. Come. As of today, it is not your uncle who gives the orders.

GASPARINA: I am coming, Husband.

(FABRIZIO *enters from his house.*)

FABRIZIO: You may be betrothed to my niece, but remember upon whom you must depend for the next ten years. And I don't want to see you throwing your money away on these people.

CAVALIER: But the supper has been prepared and paid for. Please, allow me to enjoy this one last pleasure.

FABRIZIO: If it's the last, then I allow it. But don't ask me to sit with those savages.

LUCIETTA: Oh, come on. We're sorry. When we're happy we get sort of carried away. But we don't always act like this. Sir, let's start now if you are ready.

CAVALIER: Whenever you wish.

LUCIETTA: Anzoletto, what do you say?

ANZOLETTO: It's up to you.

CATTE: Then let's do it. Courage. Courage.

ANZOLETTO: Here is my wife.

LUCIETTA: Here is my husband.

CATTE: (*To* LUCIETTA) One of these days, you'll be at my wedding.

PASQUA: I want to get married so bad I can taste it.

GNESE: I'm jealous. When's my turn?

ORSOLA: In two years.

PASQUA: Why do we have to wait two years?

GNESE: That's forever.

ORSOLA: It'll pass quickly. (GASPARINA *is back on the balcony.*)

GASPARINA: It's too crowded down there.

CAVALIER: Come down. Have some fun. It's carnival time! And in the morning, we must leave.

LUCIETTA: Gasparina, where are you going?

GASPARINA: Don't you know better than to call me by my name? Use my title.

LUCIETTA: What's your title?

GASPARINA: "Mrs". Tomorrow my husband, my uncle, and myself are going someplace worthy of us.

LUCIETTA: Best of luck.

ORSOLA: Really and truly.

CAVALIER: Come, let's go into the inn and pass the night with happy hearts. And then tomorrow, we shall say: Venice, goodbye.

(*All go into the inn;* GASPARINA *comes out of her house.*)

GASPARINA: (*Alone*)
Farewell dear dear Venice.
Farewell Venice, my sweet.
Goodbye cute campiello.
Goodbye little street.
Let's not say you're ugly,
Let's not say you're loud,
Let's only say what gives us pleasure,
Should here be allowed.

END OF COMEDY